# Lowercase Letters

a b c d e f g h i j k l m n o

p q r s t u v w x y z 1 2 3

4 5 6 7 8 9

Practice each cursive letter, then write your own.

a a a a a a a a a a a

*Practice each cursive letter, then write your own.*

*Practice each cursive letter, then write your own.*

Practice each cursive letter, then write your own.

d

D

*Practice each cursive letter, then write your own.*

Practice each cursive letter, then write your own.

*Practice each cursive letter, then write your own.*

j

J

*Practice each cursive letter, then write your own.*

Practice each cursive letter, then write your own.

*Practice each cursive letter, then write your own.*

n n n n n n n n n

n

n n n n n n n n n

n

n n n n n n n

Practice each cursive letter, then write your own.

Practice each cursive letter, then write your own.

*Practice each cursive letter, then write your own.*

Practice each cursive letter, then write your own.

t t t t t t t t t t t t

t t t t t t t t t t t t

t t t t t t t t t t t t

T T T T T T T T T T

T T T T T T T T T T

T T T T T T T T T T

*Practice each cursive letter, then write your own.*

Practice each cursive letter, then write your own.

Amendments to the Constitution of
the United States of America
Articles in addition to, and
amendment of, the Constitution of the
United States of America, proposed by
Congress, and ratified by the several
states, pursuant to the Fifth Article
of the original Constitution.

Amendments to the Constitution of
the United States of America
Articles in addition to, and
amendment of, the Constitution of the
United States of America, proposed by
Congress, and ratified by the several
states, pursuant to the Fifth Article
of the original Constitution.

Amendment 1 Religion and Expression

Congress shall make no law respecting an establishment of religion, or prohibiting the free exercise thereof; or abridging the freedom of speech, or of the press; or the right of the people peaceably to assemble, and to petition the Government for a redress of grievances.

Amendment 1 Religion and Expression

Congress shall make no law respecting an establishment of religion, or prohibiting the free exercise thereof; or abridging the freedom of speech, or of the press; or the right of the people peaceably to assemble, and to petition the Government for a redress of grievances.

Amendment 2 Bearing Arms
A well regulated Militia, being
necessary to the security of a free
State, the right of the people to keep
and bear Arms, shall not be
infringed.
Amendment 3 Quartering Soldiers
No Soldier shall, in time of peace be
quartered in any house, without the
consent of the Owner, nor in time
of war, but in a manner to be
prescribed by law.

Amendment 2 Bearing Arms
A well regulated Militia, being
necessary to the security of a free
State, the right of the people to keep
and bear Arms, shall not be
infringed.
Amendment 3 Quartering Soldiers
No Soldier shall, in time of peace be
quartered in any house, without the
consent of the Owner, nor in time
of war, but in a manner to be
prescribed by law.

Amendment 4 Search and Seizure

The right of the people to be secure in their persons, houses, papers, and effects, against unreasonable searches and seizures, shall not be violated, and no Warrants shall issue, but upon probable cause, supported by Oath or affirmation, and particularly describing the place to be searched, and the persons or things to be seized.

Amendment 4 Search and Seizure
The right of the people to be secure
in their persons, houses, papers, and
effects, against unreasonable searches
and seizures, shall not be violated,
and no Warrants shall issue, but
upon probable cause, supported by
Oath or affirmation, and
particularly describing the place to
be searched, and the persons or
things to be seized.

Amendment 5 Rights of Persons
No person shall be held to answer
for a capital, or otherwise infamous
crime, unless on a presentment or
indictment of a Grand Jury, except
in cases arising in the land or
naval forces, or in the Militia,
when in actual service in time of
War or public danger; nor shall
any person be subject for the same
offence to be twice put in jeopardy of
life or limb; nor shall be compelled
in any criminal case to be a
witness against himself, nor be
deprived of life, liberty, or property,
without due process of law; nor
shall private property be taken for

Amendment 5 Rights of Persons
No person shall be held to answer
for a capital, or otherwise infamous
crime, unless on a presentment or
indictment of a Grand Jury, except
in cases arising in the land or
naval forces, or in the Militia,
when in actual service in time of
War or public danger; nor shall
any person be subject for the same
offence to be twice put in jeopardy of
life or limb; nor shall be compelled
in any criminal case to be a
witness against himself, nor be
deprived of life, liberty, or property,
without due process of law; nor
shall private property be taken for

public use, without just
compensation.
Amendment 6 Rights of Accused
In all criminal prosecutions, the
accused shall enjoy the right to a
speedy and public trial, by an
impartial jury of the State and
district wherein the crime shall have
been committed, which district shall
have been previously ascertained by
law, and to be informed of the
nature and cause of the accusation;
to be confronted with the witnesses
against him; to have compulsory
process for obtaining witnesses in his
favor, and to have the Assistance of
Counsel for his defence.

public use, without just compensation.

Amendment 6 Rights of Accused

In all criminal prosecutions, the accused shall enjoy the right to a speedy and public trial, by an impartial jury of the State and district wherein the crime shall have been committed, which district shall have been previously ascertained by law, and to be informed of the nature and cause of the accusation; to be confronted with the witnesses against him; to have compulsory process for obtaining witnesses in his favor, and to have the Assistance of Counsel for his defence.

Amendment 7 Civil Trials

In Suits at common law, where the value in controversy shall exceed twenty dollars, the right of trial by jury shall be preserved, and no fact tried by a jury, shall be otherwise re-examined in any Court of the United States, than according to the rules of the common law.

Amendment 8 Further Guarantees in Criminal Cases

Excessive bail shall not be required, nor excessive fines imposed, nor cruel and unusual punishments inflicted.

Amendment 7 Civil Trials
In Suits at common law, where the
value in controversy shall exceed
twenty dollars, the right of trial by
jury shall be preserved, and no fact
tried by a jury, shall be otherwise
re-examined in any Court of the
United States, than according to the
rules of the common law.
Amendment 8 Further Guarantees
in Criminal Cases
Excessive bail shall not be required,
nor excessive fines imposed, nor
cruel and unusual punishments
inflicted.

Amendment 9 Unenumerated Rights
The enumeration in the Constitution,
of certain rights, shall not be
construed to deny or disparage others
retained by the people.
Amendment 10 Reserved Powers
The powers not delegated to the
United States by the Constitution,
nor prohibited by it to the States, are
reserved to the States respectively, or
to the people.

Amendment 9 Unenumerated Rights
The enumeration in the Constitution,
of certain rights, shall not be
construed to deny or disparage others
retained by the people.
Amendment 10 Reserved Powers
The powers not delegated to the
United States by the Constitution,
nor prohibited by it to the States, are
reserved to the States respectively, or
to the people.

Amendment 11 Suits Against States
The Judicial power of the United
States shall not be construed to
extend to any suit in law or equity,
commenced or prosecuted against one
of the United States by Citizens of
another State, or by Citizens or
Subjects of any Foreign State.

Amendment 11 Suits Against States
The Judicial power of the United
States shall not be construed to
extend to any suit in law or equity,
commenced or prosecuted against one
of the United States by Citizens of
another State, or by Citizens or
Subjects of any Foreign State.

Amendment 12 Election of President
The Electors shall meet in their
respective states and vote by ballot
for President and Vice-President, one
of whom, at least, shall not be an
inhabitant of the same state with
themselves; they shall name in their
ballots the person voted for as
President, and in distinct ballots the
person voted for as Vice- President,
and they shall make distinct lists of
all persons voted for as President,
and of all persons voted for as Vice-
President, and of the number of votes
for each, which lists they shall sign
and certify, and transmit sealed to
the seat of the government of the

Amendment 12 Election of President
The Electors shall meet in their
respective states and vote by ballot
for President and Vice-President, one
of whom, at least, shall not be an
inhabitant of the same state with
themselves; they shall name in their
ballots the person voted for as
President, and in distinct ballots the
person voted for as Vice-President,
and they shall make distinct lists of
all persons voted for as President,
and of all persons voted for as Vice-
President, and of the number of votes
for each, which lists they shall sign
and certify, and transmit sealed to
the seat of the government of the

United States, directed to the
President of the Senate;--The
President of the Senate shall, in the
presence of the Senate and House of
Representatives, open all the
certificates and the votes shall then
be counted;--The person having the
greatest Number of votes for
President, shall be the President, if
such number be a majority of the
whole number of Electors appointed;
and if no person have such majority,
then from the persons having the
highest numbers not exceeding three
on the list of those voted for as
President, the House of Representatives
shall choose immediately, by ballot,

United States, directed to the
President of the Senate;---The
President of the Senate shall, in the
presence of the Senate and House of
Representatives, open all the
certificates and the votes shall then
be counted;---The person having the
greatest Number of votes for
President, shall be the President, if
such number be a majority of the
whole number of Electors appointed;
and if no person have such majority
then from the persons having the
highest numbers not exceeding three
on the list of those voted for as
President, the House of Representatives
shall choose immediately, by ballot,

the President. But in choosing the President, the votes shall be taken by states, the representation from each state having one vote; a quorum for this purpose shall consist of a member or members from two-thirds of the states, and a majority of all the states shall be necessary to a choice. And if the House of Representatives shall not choose a President whenever the right of choice shall devolve upon them, before the fourth day of March next following, then the Vice- President shall act as President, as in the case of the death or other constitutional disability of the President--The person having the

the President. But in choosing the
President, the votes shall be taken by
states, the representation from each
state having one vote; a quorum for
this purpose shall consist of a
member or members from two-thirds
of the states, and a majority of all
the states shall be necessary to a
choice. And if the House of
Representatives shall not choose a
President whenever the right of choice
shall devolve upon them, before the
fourth day of March next following,
then the Vice-- President shall act as
President, as in the case of the death
or other constitutional disability of
the President----The person having the

greatest number of votes as Vice-President, shall be the Vice-President, if such number be a majority of the whole number of Electors appointed, and if no person have a majority, then from the two highest numbers on the list, the Senate shall choose the Vice-President; a quorum for the purpose shall consist of two-thirds of the whole number of Senators, and a majority of the whole number shall be necessary to a choice. But no person constitutionally ineligible to the office of President shall be eligible to that of Vice-President of the United States.

greatest number of votes as Vice-President, shall be the Vice-President, if such number be a majority of the whole number of Electors appointed, and if no person have a majority, then from the two highest numbers on the list, the Senate shall choose the Vice-President; a quorum for the purpose shall consist of two-thirds of the whole number of Senators, and a majority of the whole number shall be necessary to a choice. But no person constitutionally ineligible to the office of President shall be eligible to that of Vice-President of the United States.

Amendment 13 Slavery and Involuntary Servitude

Section 1.

Neither slavery nor involuntary servitude, except as a punishment for crime whereof the party shall have been duly convicted, shall exist within the United States, or any place subject to their jurisdiction.

Section 2.

Congress shall have power to enforce this article by appropriate legislation.

Amendment 13 Slavery and
Involuntary Servitude
Section 1.
Neither slavery nor involuntary
servitude, except as a punishment for
crime whereof the party shall have
been duly convicted, shall exist
within the United States, or any
place subject to their jurisdiction.
Section 2.
Congress shall have power to enforce
this article by appropriate legislation.

Amendment 14 Rights Guaranteed, Privileges and Immunities of Citizenship, Due Process and Equal Protection Section. 1

All persons born or naturalized in the United States and subject to the jurisdiction thereof, are citizens of the United States and of the State wherein they reside. No State shall make or enforce any law which shall abridge the privileges or immunities of citizens of the United States; nor shall any State deprive any person of life, liberty, or property, without due process of law; nor deny to any person within its jurisdiction the equal protection of the laws.

Amendment 14 Rights Guaranteed, Privileges and Immunities of Citizenship, Due Process and Equal Protection Section. 1

All persons born or naturalized in the United States and subject to the jurisdiction thereof, are citizens of the United States and of the State wherein they reside. No State shall make or enforce any law which shall abridge the privileges or immunities of citizens of the United States; nor shall any State deprive any person of life, liberty, or property, without due process of law; nor deny to any person within its jurisdiction the equal protection of the laws.

Section. 2.
Representatives shall be apportioned among the several States according to their respective numbers, counting the whole number of persons in each State, excluding Indians not taxed. But when the right to vote at any election for the choice of electors for President and Vice President of the United States, Representatives in Congress, the Executive and Judicial officers of a State, or the members of the Legislature thereof, is denied to any of the male inhabitants of such State, being twenty-one years of age, and citizens of the United States, or in any way abridged, except for

Section. 2.
Representatives shall be apportioned among the several States according to their respective numbers, counting the whole number of persons in each State, excluding Indians not taxed. But when the right to vote at any election for the choice of electors for President and Vice President of the United States, Representatives in Congress, the Executive and Judicial officers of a State, or the members of the Legislature thereof, is denied to any of the male inhabitants of such State, being twenty-one years of age, and citizens of the United States, or in any way abridged, except for

participation in rebellion, or other
crime, the basis of representation
therein shall be reduced in the
proportion which the number of such
male citizens shall bear to the whole
number of male citizens twenty-one
years of age in such State.

Section. 3.
No person shall be a Senator or
Representative in Congress, or elector
of President and Vice President, or
hold any office, civil or military,
under the United States, or under
any State, who, having previously
taken an oath, as a member of
Congress, or as an officer of the

participation in rebellion, or other crime, the basis of representation therein shall be reduced in the proportion which the number of such male citizens shall bear to the whole number of male citizens twenty-one years of age in such State.

Section. 3.

No person shall be a Senator or Representative in Congress, or elector of President and Vice President, or hold any office, civil or military, under the United States, or under any State, who, having previously taken an oath, as a member of Congress, or as an officer of the

United States, or as a member of any State legislature, or as an executive or judicial officer of any State, to support the Constitution of the United States, shall have engaged in insurrection or rebellion against the same, or given aid or comfort to the enemies thereof. But Congress may by a vote of two-thirds of each House, remove such disability.

Section. 4.

The validity of the public debt of the United States, authorized by law, including debts incurred for payment of pensions and bounties for services in suppressing insurrection or

United States, or as a member of
any State legislature, or as an
executive or judicial officer of any
State, to support the Constitution of
the United States, shall have engaged
in insurrection or rebellion against
the same, or given aid or comfort to
the enemies thereof. But Congress
may by a vote of two-thirds of each
House, remove such disability.

Section. 4.
The validity of the public debt of the
United States, authorized by law,
including debts incurred for payment
of pensions and bounties for services
in suppressing insurrection or

rebellion, shall not be questioned. But neither the United States nor any State shall assume or pay any debt or obligation incurred in aid of insurrection or rebellion against the United States, or any claim for the loss or emancipation of any slave; but all such debts, obligations and claims shall be held illegal and void.

Section. 5.
The Congress shall have power to enforce, by appropriate legislation, the provisions of this article.

rebellion, shall not be questioned. But neither the United States nor any State shall assume or pay any debt or obligation incurred in aid of insurrection or rebellion against the United States, or any claim for the loss or emancipation of any slave; but all such debts, obligations and claims shall be held illegal and void.

Section. 5.
The Congress shall have power to enforce, by appropriate legislation, the provisions of this article.

# Amendment 15 Right of Citizens to Vote

## Section. 1

The right of citizens of the United States to vote shall not be denied or abridged by the United States or by any State on account of race, color, or previous condition of servitude.

## Section. 2

The Congress shall have power to enforce this article by appropriate legislation.

Amendment 15 Right of Citizens to Vote

Section. 1

The right of citizens of the United States to vote shall not be denied or abridged by the United States or by any State on account of race, color, or previous condition of servitude.

Section. 2

The Congress shall have power to enforce this article by appropriate legislation.

Amendment 16 Income Tax
The Congress shall have power to lay
and collect taxes on incomes, from
whatever source derived, without
apportionment among the several
States, and without regard to any
census or enumeration.

Amendment 16 Income Tax
The Congress shall have power to lay
and collect taxes on incomes, from
whatever source derived, without
apportionment among the several
States, and without regard to any
census or enumeration.

Amendment 17 Popular Election of Senators

The Senate of the United States shall be composed of two Senators from each State, elected by the people thereof, for six years; and each Senator shall have one vote. The electors in each State shall have the qualifications requisite for electors of the most numerous branch of the State legislatures.

When vacancies happen in the representation of any State in the Senate, the executive authority of such State shall issue writs of election to fill such vacancies:

Amendment 17 Popular Election of
Senators

The Senate of the United States shall
be composed of two Senators from
each State, elected by the people
thereof, for six years; and each
Senator shall have one vote. The
electors in each State shall have the
qualifications requisite for electors of
the most numerous branch of the
State legislatures.

When vacancies happen in the
representation of any State in the
Senate, the executive authority of
such State shall issue writs of
election to fill such vacancies:

Provided, That the legislature of any State may empower the executive thereof to make temporary appointments until the people fill the vacancies by election as the legislature may direct.

This amendment shall not be so construed as to affect the election or term of any Senator chosen before it becomes valid as part of the Constitution.

Provided, That the legislature of any State may empower the executive thereof to make temporary appointments until the people fill the vacancies by election as the legislature may direct.

This amendment shall not be so construed as to affect the election or term of any Senator chosen before it becomes valid as part of the Constitution.

Amendment 18 Prohibition of Intoxicating Liquors

Section. 1

After one year from the ratification of this article the manufacture, sale, or transportation of intoxicating liquors within, the importation thereof into, or the exportation thereof from the United States and all territory subject to the jurisdiction thereof for beverage purposes is hereby prohibited.

Sec. 2

The Congress and the several States shall have concurrent power to enforce this article by appropriate legislation.

Amendment 18 Prohibition of
Intoxicating Liquors
Section. 1
After one year from the ratification
of this article the manufacture, sale,
or transportation of intoxicating
liquors within, the importation
thereof into, or the exportation thereof
from the United States and all
territory subject to the jurisdiction
thereof for beverage purposes is hereby
prohibited.
Sec. 2
The Congress and the several States
shall have concurrent power to
enforce this article by appropriate
legislation.

Sec. 3 This article shall be
inoperative unless it shall have been
ratified as an amendment to the
Constitution by the legislatures of the
several States, as provided in the
Constitution, within seven years
from the date of the submission
hereof to the States by the Congress.

Sec. 3 This article shall be
inoperative unless it shall have been
ratified as an amendment to the
Constitution by the legislatures of the
several States, as provided in the
Constitution, within seven years
from the date of the submission
hereof to the States by the Congress.

Amendment 19 Women's Suffrage
Rights
The right of citizens of the United
States to vote shall not be denied or
abridged by the United States or by
any State on account of sex. Congress
shall have power to enforce this
article by appropriate legislation.

Amendment 19 Women's Suffrage
Rights
The right of citizens of the United
States to vote shall not be denied or
abridged by the United States or by
any State on account of sex. Congress
shall have power to enforce this
article by appropriate legislation.

Amendment 20 Commencement of the Terms of President, Vice President, and Members of Congress

Section. 1. The terms of the President and Vice President shall end at noon on the 20th day of January, and the terms of Senators and Representatives at noon on the 3d day of January, of the years in which such terms would have ended if this article had not been ratified; and the terms of their successors shall then begin.

Sec. 2. The Congress shall assemble at least once in every year, and such meeting shall begin at noon on the 3d day of January, unless they

Amendment 20 Commencement of the Terms of President, Vice President, and Members of Congress

Section. 1. The terms of the President and Vice President shall end at noon on the 20th day of January, and the terms of Senators and Representatives at noon on the 3d day of January, of the years in which such terms would have ended if this article had not been ratified; and the terms of their successors shall then begin.

Sec. 2. The Congress shall assemble at least once in every year, and such meeting shall begin at noon on the 3d day of January, unless they

shall by law appoint a different day.

Sec. 3. If, at the time fixed for the beginning of the term of the President, the President elect shall have died, the Vice President elect shall become President. If a President shall not have been chosen before the time fixed for the beginning of his term, or if the President elect shall have failed to qualify, then the Vice President elect shall act as President until a President shall have qualified; and the Congress may by law provide for the case wherein neither a President elect nor a Vice President elect shall have qualified, shall by law appoint a different day.

Sec. 3. If, at the time fixed for the beginning of the term of the President, the President elect shall have died, the Vice President elect shall become President. If a President shall not have been chosen before the time fixed for the beginning of his term, or if the President elect shall have failed to qualify, then the Vice President elect shall act as President until a President shall have qualified; and the Congress may by law provide for the case wherein neither a President elect nor a Vice President elect shall have qualified,

declaring who shall then act as President, or the manner in which one who is to act shall be selected, and such person shall act accordingly until a President or Vice President shall have qualified.

Sec. 4. The Congress may by law provide for the case of the death of any of the persons from whom the House of Representatives may choose a President whenever the right of choice shall have devolved upon them, and for the case of the death of any of the persons from whom the Senate may choose a Vice President whenever the right of choice

declaring who shall then act as
President, or the manner in which
one who is to act shall be selected,
and such person shall act
accordingly until a President or
Vice President shall have qualified.

Sec. 4. The Congress may by law
provide for the case of the death of
any of the persons from whom the
House of Representatives may choose
a President whenever the right of
choice shall have devolved upon
them, and for the case of the death
of any of the persons from whom
the Senate may choose a Vice
President whenever the right of choice

shall have devolved upon them.

Sec. 5. Sections 1 and 2 shall take effect on the 15th day of October following the ratification of this article.

Sec. 6. This article shall be inoperative unless it shall have been ratified as an amendment to the Constitution by the legislatures of three-fourths of the several States within seven years from the date of its submission.

shall have devolved upon them.

Sec. 5. Sections 1 and 2 shall take effect on the 15th day of October following the ratification of this article.

Sec. 6. This article shall be inoperative unless it shall have been ratified as an amendment to the Constitution by the legislatures of three-fourths of the several States within seven years from the date of its submission.

Amendment 21 Repeal of the Eighteenth Amendment

Section. 1. The eighteenth article of amendment to the Constitution of the United States is hereby repealed.

Sec. 2. The transportation or importation into any State, Territory, or possession of the United States for delivery or use therein of intoxicating liquors, in violation of the laws thereof, is hereby prohibited.

Sec. 3. This article shall be inoperative unless it shall have been ratified as an amendment to the Constitution by conventions in the several States, as provided in the Constitution, within seven years

Amendment 21 Repeal of the
Eighteenth Amendment
Section. 1. The eighteenth article of
amendment to the Constitution of
the United States is hereby repealed.
Sec. 2. The transportation or
importation into any State,
Territory, or possession of the United
States for delivery or use therein of
intoxicating liquors, in violation of
the laws thereof, is hereby prohibited.
Sec. 3. This article shall be
inoperative unless it shall have been
ratified as an amendment to the
Constitution by conventions in the
several States, as provided in the
Constitution, within seven years

from the date of the submission hereof to the States by the Congress. Amendment 22 Presidential Tenure Section. 1. No person shall be elected to the office of the President more than twice, and no person who has held the office of President, or acted as President, for more than two years of a term to which some other person was elected President shall be elected to the office of the President more than once. But this Article shall not apply to any person holding the office of President, when this Article was proposed by the Congress, and shall not prevent any person who may be holding the

from the date of the submission
hereof to the States by the Congress.
Amendment 22 Presidential Tenure
Section. 1. No person shall be elected
to the office of the President more
than twice, and no person who has
held the office of President, or acted
as President, for more than two
years of a term to which some other
person was elected President shall be
elected to the office of the President
more than once. But this Article
shall not apply to any person
holding the office of President, when
this Article was proposed by the
Congress, and shall not prevent any
person who may be holding the

office of President, or acting as President, during the term within which this Article becomes operative from holding the office of President or acting as President during the remainder of such term.

Sec. 2. This article shall be inoperative unless it shall have been ratified as an amendment to the Constitution by the legislatures of three-fourths of the several States within seven years from the date of its submission to the States by the Congress.

office of President, or acting as President, during the term within which this Article becomes operative from holding the office of President or acting as President during the remainder of such term.

Sec. 2. This article shall be inoperative unless it shall have been ratified as an amendment to the Constitution by the legislatures of three-fourths of the several States within seven years from the date of its submission to the States by the Congress.

Amendment 23 Presidential Electors
for the District of Columbia
Section. 1. The District constituting
the seat of Government of the
United States shall appoint in such
manner as the Congress may direct:
A number of electors of President
and Vice President equal to the
whole number of Senators and
Representatives in Congress to which
the District would be entitled if it
were a State, but in no event more
than the least populous State; they
shall be in addition to those
appointed by the States, but they
shall be considered, for the purposes
of the election of President and Vice

Amendment 23 Presidential Electors
for the District of Columbia
Section. 1. The District constituting
the seat of Government of the
United States shall appoint in such
manner as the Congress may direct:
A number of electors of President
and Vice President equal to the
whole number of Senators and
Representatives in Congress to which
the District would be entitled if it
were a State, but in no event more
than the least populous State; they
shall be in addition to those
appointed by the States, but they
shall be considered, for the purposes
of the election of President and Vice

President, to be electors appointed by a State; and they shall meet in the District and perform such duties as provided by the twelfth article of amendment.

Sec. 2. The Congress shall have power to enforce this article by appropriate legislation.

President, to be electors appointed by
a State; and they shall meet in the
District and perform such duties as
provided by the twelfth article of
amendment.
Sec. 2. The Congress shall have
power to enforce this article by
appropriate legislation.

Amendment 24 Abolition of the Poll Tax Qualification in Federal Elections

Section. 1. The right of citizens of the United States to vote in any primary or other election for President or Vice President, for electors for President or Vice President, or for Senator or Representative in Congress, shall not be denied or abridged by the United States or any State by reason of failure to pay any poll tax or other tax.

Section. 2. The Congress shall have power to enforce this article by appropriate legislation.

Amendment 24 Abolition of the Poll Tax Qualification in Federal Elections

Section 1. The right of citizens of the United States to vote in any primary or other election for President or Vice President, for electors for President or Vice President, or for Senator or Representative in Congress, shall not be denied or abridged by the United States or any State by reason of failure to pay any poll tax or other tax.

Section 2. The Congress shall have power to enforce this article by appropriate legislation.

Amendment 25 Presidential
Vacancy, Disability, or Incapacity
Section. 1. In case of the removal
of the President from office or of his
death or resignation, the Vice
President shall become President.
Section. 2. Whenever there is a
vacancy in the office of the Vice
President, the President shall
nominate a Vice President who shall
take office upon confirmation by a
majority vote of both Houses of
Congress.
Section. 3. Whenever the President
transmits to the President pro
tempore of the Senate and the
Speaker of the House of

Amendment 25 Presidential
Vacancy, Disability, or Incapacity
Section. 1. In case of the removal
of the President from office or of his
death or resignation, the Vice
President shall become President.
Section. 2. Whenever there is a
vacancy in the office of the Vice
President, the President shall
nominate a Vice President who shall
take office upon confirmation by a
majority vote of both Houses of
Congress.
Section. 3. Whenever the President
transmits to the President pro
tempore of the Senate and the
Speaker of the House of

Representatives his written declaration that he is unable to discharge the powers and duties of his office, and until he transmits to them a written declaration to the contrary, such powers and duties shall be discharged by the Vice President as Acting President.

Section. 4. Whenever the Vice President and a majority of either the principal officers of the executive departments or of such other body as Congress may by law provide, transmit to the President pro tempore of the Senate and the Speaker of the House of Representatives their written

Representatives his written
declaration that he is unable to
discharge the powers and duties of
his office, and until he transmits to
them a written declaration to the
contrary, such powers and duties
shall be discharged by the Vice
President as Acting President.
Section. 4. Whenever the Vice
President and a majority of either
the principal officers of the executive
departments or of such other body
as Congress may by law provide,
transmit to the President pro
tempore of the Senate and the
Speaker of the House of
Representatives their written

declaration that the President is
unable to discharge the powers and
duties of his office, the Vice President
shall immediately assume the
powers and duties of the office as
Acting President.
Thereafter, when the President
transmits to the President pro
tempore of the Senate and the
Speaker of the House of
Representatives has written
declaration that no inability exists,
he shall resume the powers and
duties of his office unless the Vice
President and a majority of either
the principal officers of the executive
department or of such other body as

declaration that the President is
unable to discharge the powers and
duties of his office, the Vice President
shall immediately assume the
powers and duties of the office as
Acting President.
Thereafter, when the President
transmits to the President pro
tempore of the Senate and the
Speaker of the House of
Representatives his written
declaration that no inability exists,
he shall resume the powers and
duties of his office unless the Vice
President and a majority of either
the principal officers of the executive
department or of such other body as

vote of both Houses that the President is unable to discharge the powers and duties of his office, the Vice President shall continue to discharge the same as Acting President; otherwise, the President shall resume the powers and duties of his office.

vote of both Houses that the President is unable to discharge the powers and duties of his office, the Vice President shall continue to discharge the same as Acting President; otherwise, the President shall resume the powers and duties of his office.

# Amendment 26 Reduction of Voting Age Qualification

Section. 1. The right of citizens of the United States, who are eighteen years of age or older, to vote shall not be denied or abridged by the United States or by any State on account of age.

Section. 2. The Congress shall have power to enforce this article by appropriate legislation.

Amendment 26 Reduction of Voting Age Qualification

Section. 1. The right of citizens of the United States, who are eighteen years of age or older, to vote shall not be denied or abridged by the United States or by any State on account of age.

Section. 2. The Congress shall have power to enforce this article by appropriate legislation.

Amendment 26 Reduction of Voting Age Qualification

Section. 1. The right of citizens of the United States, who are eighteen years of age or older, to vote shall not be denied or abridged by the United States or by any State on account of age.

Section. 2. The Congress shall have power to enforce this article by appropriate legislation.

Amendment 27 Congressional Pay

No law varying the compensation for the services of the Senators and Representatives shall take effect, until an election of Representatives shall have intervened.

Amendment 26 Reduction of Voting Age Qualification

Section. 1. The right of citizens of the United States, who are eighteen years of age or older, to vote shall not be denied or abridged by the United States or by any State on account of age.

Section. 2. The Congress shall have power to enforce this article by appropriate legislation.

Amendment 27 Congressional Pay

No law varying the compensation for the services of the Senators and Representatives shall take effect, until an election of Representatives shall have intervened.